LOVE POEMS AND DEATH THREATS

a collection of poetry by

SAMUEL WAGAN WATSON

UQP

Hailing from honourable ancestors of the Birri-Gubba, Mununjali, Germanic and Gaelic peoples, Samuel Wagan Watson grew up in a family of accomplished authors, political players, entrepreneurs, academics, artists and raconteurs. His collection of poetry *Of Muse, Meandering and Midnight* won the 1999 David Unaipon prize for unpublished Indigenous writers. Since then he has written four more collections: *Itinerant Blues* (2001); *Hotel Bone* (2001, Vagabond Press); *Smoke Encrypted Whispers* (2004), which won the New South Wales Premier's Book of the Year and the Kenneth Slessor Prize; and *The Curse Words* (2011, Vagabond Press). His work has been translated into seven languages, inspired various musical compositions, and been the subject of film and television productions and visual art projects. In 2018 Samuel was awarded the Patrick White Literary Award.

Love Poems and Death Threats won the 2016 Scanlon Award for Indigenous Poetry and was shortlisted for the Adelaide Festival Awards for Literature.

PRAISE FOR *LOVE POEMS AND DEATH THREATS*

'*Love Poems and Death Threats* truly sung my soul.' Maxine Beneba Clark, *Sydney Morning Herald*

'A great collection from a poet "mapping the songlines": inventive, satirical, tender.' *Australian Book Review*

'A triumph: a gathering of emotional endurance and experience. An extremely rewarding book from an important and fascinating Australian voice.' *Writ Poetry Review*

This collection is dedicated to the people I love,
and the ones who have almost done me in.

CONTENTS

I. BLOOD AND INK

II. NO STANDING ANYTIME

III. NO NAKED FLAMES

I. BLOOD AND INK

BLOOD AND INK

For Uncle Ross

'Blood, Herr Reiss, can never be eradicated like ink.'
– Philip K. Dick, *The Man in the High Castle*

i. Headwaters

'I AM A RIVER ...'
How your words reverberate off the mirror of our conscience. The connection is water. Wanting to pour forth the bubbling within. A well of knowledge, waiting below the surface of us all.

And as you professed, my uncle, we all congregated. Albeit in a dark hour, we dreamed as one, in a pure breast of afternoon light. There were tears, but they were merely spray off the surface of your departure. Young sea eagles danced your wake.

What you gave us cannot be taught in foreign halls; the darkness of humanity and poison pens. How they fashion textbooks to suit the tides of chaos.

Ink can be cleansed in the headwaters of your flow. Wash my eyes from censored images of history. I am not a neo-human of dystopia.

Below your river a dangerous undertow can gather momentum and try to pull us down.

But we will always float as estuaries in your memory, a consensus of blood that can never be eradicated like ink.

ii. Ebb tide

There is no recession in your departure. The river replenishes and everyone needs time to regain buoyancy. We have to catch our breath and wade.

You taught us never to dive 'headfirst' into unknown depths. Feel the water as each one of us is our own burgeoning course.

There will be low water succeeding at times, but we will always try to maintain a steady drift. And in the ebb tide – as your decree, my teacher – no one should be left behind.

Question all questions drowned and forgotten. In their resuscitations, storm birds break glass and fish shed tears. In a consensus of dreams, everything could surface.

iii. Backwaters

As a pupil I must ask: How is it you charted the backwaters before your time? Is it connected with the Dawson River, the conduit of your mother's spring? I am uncharted of the Kungulu ways in my being.

I have smelt the burnt husks of brigalow leaves and twine, as we have now entwined, in the backwaters of your journey. No heart of darkness has rested here. The river does not rest.

What I search for is further upstream, in an essence, the midst of unexplored waters. A whirlpool simpatico belongs there; unrest and calm.

iv. Postscript in a bottle

Uncle, will you please make a beacon; a campfire on the shore of our backwaters? I fear some of us could lose our way …

The river will never rest, our collective thoughts from the headwaters, through the ebb tide and into the backwaters of our being. We are all rivers, on a discourse of ink and blood …

Kungulu – Great-Granny Watson's language group in Central Queensland.
Brigalow is a sacred tree of my honourable ancestors.

IN THE LIGHT OF TWO FIRES

i.

(The state archives reveal too much, circa 1996)
My eyes trawl depressions created by ink.
I am able to navigate sinkholes
                    void of humanity.
Lines of ignorance and contradiction
                    proud factotums of brutality.
And these documents are not even a century young,
authored by a monster, claiming to be a 'Protector of
  Aborigines'.

  My great-great-granny is constantly referred to as a 'gin',
  her piccaninnies are traded like cattle;
  this is the commodification of my blood.
  There are no romantic tales in these pages
  just itemised accounts of my kin's value
                    in pounds and shillings.
These are the wages of war and fear.

ii.

(A morning of dark horses, circa 1907)
Hooves stab a ground that dawn barely touched.
A little boy is ripped from the camp, his mother a widow.
Mourning-stench flakes everything already and soon flames
  of sorrow
                    will bear ashes again.
A swift sulky is driven by a black-robe of god.
Another horse is mounted by a black-robe of the gun.

The infant is barrelled into the nightmare of servitude
the infinite career of horrors.
I am named after this child, and he will never be civilised
like this again.
We've never used the word 'stolen' at home,
but the term hardly surmises our history.
Echoes of screams shared by mother and son;
from warm maternal provisions, into a furnace
the slave-master's wrath.
Journey into limbo; between the
light of two fires.

APOCALYPTIC QUATRAINS: THE AUSTRALIAN WHEAT BOARD/IRAQ BRIBERY SCANDAL

> 'The call of the strange bird is heard
> on the pipe of the breathing floor;
> so high will become the bushels of wheat
> that man will cannibalise his fellow man …'
> – Nostradamus, II:75

We learn, yet forget, in the cataclysm of our birth
the owl songs of Muk-Muk;
the death feather, and reacquainted we shall be
in the sunset of our mortality.

(The call of the strange bird is heard …)

The didjeridu sits in the corner of my room
near the window, ghosts breathe
my frailty of spirit
resonates in the acoustics of this gouged plain.

(… on the pipe of the breathing floor …)

The dark skin ripped apart
perished seeds of the Dreamtime
to the new crops of the invader
blood furrows this occupied soil of neo-pestilence.

(… so high will become the bushels of wheat …)

Harvested by the demon-seed of the invader
and grain-fed the insatiable hunger of the dictator
they danced, until caught red-handed
the hands bite the hands that have fed them.

(… that man will cannibalise his fellow man.)

THE GROUNDING SENTENCE

> 'On Friday, Rockhampton Magistrates Court heard that [a male], 17, had been driving around with an air gun looking to "shoot an Aboriginal person" on Australia Day ...'
>
> – 'Stung teen shot in back', *The Sunday Mail*, 29 January 2006

i.

It has been an eternity of dispersal. Knowledge, secret and sacred ... my people have become the most written about indigenous nations of the world ... but are any of those words valuable? The world my children inherit is a scattered plain; the earth is flat and often void of the echoes of their elders. For too long I have listened to the wind as it is spoken by passing semitrailers and luxury cars. For too long I have complacently existed on these killing fields and built a house of straw in the down-wind of the enemy. My ancestors' tongues are sealed and delivered trophies on the shelves of the invader's sterile museums ... for too long I have permitted the hunter inside of me to become the hunted.

Australians all let us rejoice, for we are young and free ...

ii.

From the southern banks of the Brisbane River my Mununjali blood flows south. My Birri-Gubba blood is far in the north, on the Dawson River, another river, another world away. Worlds swept with the changing winds of successive hunting regulations and administrations. From the moment we are born we are taught who we are and where we cannot go, but to be out of range is the safest place to be, no matter where your blood flows. Open game and fair game are two hearts of darkness that beat as one. The skin of the country is branded deep with crosshairs and warning signs.

A sunburnt country
land of extreme prejudice
advance Australia where?

iii.

I have hunted for trophies of my own and fallen into the snares of what the invader prides most of all, and that is the ability to turn blood against blood. There is nothing noble about becoming a savage in the despair of your own people … I am the most ignorant savage of them all … I cannot interpret the words of my Dreaming.

I cannot fly straight
a reluctant boomerang
my grounding sentence

Mununjali refers to my nan's tribe in the Beaudesert region.
Birri-Gubba refers to my pop's tribe on the central Queensland coast.

SENTINEL

The midden remains; a material witness on a promontory or beachhead over the expanses of epoch and aeon, where tributes were held in worship of richer seasons. Festivities – not so dionysian in revelry – but more rainbow-serpentine in respect, these ceremonial milestones that would acknowledge the midden a monument to a spiritual pathos of economical sharing. Sharing and nurturing; graces now almost driven from this land.

The midden remains, where elements once convened in the most sacred of communions – earth, water, fire and wind – mused in the easy linguistics of sea breeze, tongues lathered with salt. Feast and dream the prosperity of the lucky and chosen peoples, custodians in the world of the living and plenty.

The midden remains, but the sea is threatened, the earth torn, the fires exhausted, and the sky tarnished, the people scattered. Conquerors look upon you as a 'trash heap' and not a factotum from an ochre Babylon. You, the treasured 'debitage', are preyed upon by roads, skyscrapers and desecration. Your selected bones and matrix of lithium flakes are indecipherable in the wake of the newcomers' ignorance. The shells in your structure form the unworn necklace of ghosts, held together by songlines locked in an obscure servitude of silence.

The midden remains; guardian to memory.
The midden remains sacred.
The midden remains, sentinel.

HALLOWED GROUND

for Heli

Saturday morning on Logan Road and my lady is pelting me with warm little marbles from her throat: *You don't want to go anywhere, you just want to go home!*

I pull into a parking spot, fast! Her beautiful little frame; a classic Scandinavian face that just lights up in wonder … *Are you taking me to a café?*

> Dinosaurs are buried here with the remains of their tracks; this place was once only known as Central.
>
> This place was where my mum and dad had their first kiss on the tram!
>
> The café is called Hallowed Grounds and it suits. 'Make Coffee … Not War!' sign sits in the window.
>
> Mum and Dad were both arrested during the Vietnam debacle … it's Dad's birthday and we just bought him a Black Panther Party T-shirt, so this is very fitting …

You're very distant, I'm told. But, I'm very HERE, this is my factory wall and I am a local pogue!

Mt Gravatt Central takes me into her girth, a mother of all crossroads, but the only one I've walked without feeling the cattle grid of a devil.

The ectoplasm-reminder of the giant echidna who slumbers in Mt Gravatt behind us brain-locks me … the smell of good coffee and food, and *service with a smile!* I can actually dig this environment. It is humanity un-trapped. And it almost seems criminal to make a cell-call here.

Sharing a freshly squeezed juice over a *Wonder Woman* comic with good service … I am in love … I am not distant at all … I am at home … I move across the table and attempt a kiss … in my blindside a police car rolls by … everything is in order again … her lips taste like fresh life … I am safe from chaos for the time being, comfortable in these *Hallowed Grounds.*

BIRD-SONG OF IMMINENT DEATH

Death songs off the Logan Road night;
        and on the news, Blackhawks falling over Afghanistan.
Muk-Muk; the death-bird, aptly named by my elders,
                because Muk-Muk only appears to those
                        who will soon be grieving.
Muk-Muk is as metronomically challenged as the curlew,
                another death-threat-carrying kindred,
but on this particular night I clearly hear Muk-Muk's
    cuckoo-like tome.
Muk-Muk is a 'roadie' on a blackened stage
                testing sound-equipment for a phantom audience.

Hoo-Hoo!
Hoo-Hoo!
Testing, 1, 2!
Testing, 1, 2!
Hoo-Hoo!
Hoo-Hoo!

Muk-Muk sings,
                a gecko chirps
                                and an ambulance siren wails!
Darkness comes to life, ironically, drowning out the death calls.

A light rain then douses everything,
                but soon, Muk-Muk begins his final encore.
I wander out onto the patio as my girlfriend sleeps,
                I wonder of my brother's safety in Afghanistan.

The flight path culls short over the house,
and soon a storm of aluminium mullets runs a
heavenly gutter,
the flight path is so close
it seems I could catch the red-eye from Sydney
by just raising my hand.

Swing low a freedom-bird for my brother,
and low-altitude traffic, to keep the
death-bird at bay.

TERROR

'… You talk about terror … I've been terrorized all my days!'
– Willie King, 'Terrorized'

All the signs read, SMILE … YOU'RE ON CAMERA welcome to no-man's-land, you're standing on terra firma, that some explorer once dubbed Terra Australis, and then another termed terra nullius, that stole this land's dreams. Terra firma could be the next target in the War on Terror, from Terra Australis, to anti-terror laws. SMILE … YOU'RE ON CAMERA welcome to no-man's-land, Terra Australis, with its terra firma, deemed terra nullius, embroiled in the War on Terror and everyone is governed by anti-terror laws. SMILE … YOU'RE ON CAMERA welcome to no-man's-land, population under observation, you gotta love a sunburnt country with a dry, split personality. Terra Australis, under terra nullius, right where you're standing on terra firma with its beauty and its *terror, terror, terror* … welcome to no-man's-land.

KISSING GHOSTS

When dreaming
you attempt to walk on eggshells
and end up knee deep in ectoplasm,
kissing ghosts.
When yearning
you attempt not to repeat the past
yet achieve the sensation of a haunting déjà vu,
kissing ghosts.
When content
you attempt to quell a burning,
douse your mortal coil that can only be quenched while
kissing ghosts,
kissing ghosts that cannot harm you,
kissing ghosts that are not culpable for telling you they love you,
kissing ghosts that were never there,
the ectoplasm of lust a finger's length in darkness

when really,
it was all in your head.

THROW SALT

My elders are well acquainted with the unlucky,
and they acknowledge death by his sign,
don't cross a knife and fork on the kitchen table
'cause you're just inviting the devil to dine,
throw salt.

An owl is the foul feather of premonition,
black cat only eyes black times,
as red-eyed dogs prowl the Mission crossroads and hills
when bat-wings speak easy moonshine,
throw salt.

For what ails us there is cod-liver oil,
speak of the dead and it'll curve your spine,
leave a protective glass of water on night's windowsill,
gambling on the Sabbath will send you blind,
throw salt.

Touch wood and throw salt over your shoulder,
throw it once a day and make it divine,
to be superstitious is to be one with god and dark nature,
to be superstitious is to be sublime,

throw salt,
throw salt,
throw salt.

SCRATCHED

When I was a kid the weekend started with cartoons … somewhere between *Land of the Lost* and *Scooby-Doo* they'd feature 'Turf Talk with Andy Stevens'. Hearing his throaty-drawl of racing tips would set the pace of the day … the sun even seemed different on the weekend … there's no animosity in it on a Saturday … this was part of the ether of our childhood.

After breakfast we'd visit Nan and Pop and sometimes Nan's mum, Granny Roberts, would be there and then there'd be trips to the TAB and footy-club raffles and hot-dogs … a 50-cent piece seemed the size of a dinner plate … (race-calls – the nerve gas of the working class).

My cousin-brothers would visit too and we'd climb trees. Black wattle mainly; Mt Gravatt East was black wattle soil and the twisted trunks were good for conditioning little black bare-feet. We'd look out over the suburb … take in the fumes of race-calls … a kind of cloud of white-noise that was nerve gas to a blackfulla … Dad, Uncle Steve and Nan could be heard … Dad and Uncle Steve whacking their thighs with imaginary whips, *Ssss … Ssss … Ssss!* a staccato; Nan chanting, *Yes, yes, yes … ah begga that horse!* … I wanted a bike for Christmas, I wanted a *Star Wars* figure for Christmas … I wanted to be Pavlov for Christmas, just once, as the race-caller … making adults stop and listen when we kids had something trivial to say … but then you grow up and Saturday loses its magic and you understand that Saturday is only as magic as what you put into it, 'cause the whole week is a race, life is a race … and in time, Saturday just gets scratched …

IN MY MOTHER'S '80S KITCHEN

The golden light at 5am was that of a Renaissance painting,
da Vinci's code dawns after the bedtime influence
of *Cheech & Chong*,
awake, I watched junjurries dance through fingers of sun
slowly hoovering a linoleum floor.

A residue of mint from the garden by the back door
always stays with you, and a soundtrack of early morning
  traffic,
Wayne 'The Poo' Roberts crackling on the radio.

But you just couldn't fire if it was a raining Monday.
Bob Geldof telling me why I shouldn't go to school!
A shadow of politics over the kitchen table
just being a black kid, in a black family
the black-pudding of nature
racism and its insatiable appetite.

And it just made you hungry, climbing into your lunchbox
  for safety,
telling me from my mother's kitchen,
to open the mind of my pallet;
biting hard
    a bitter tongue …

Junjurries are small nymphs of Indigenous lore.

THE ALPHABET OF FISH

My brothers once showed me the bounty that could be had in bait nets. We were able to catch garfish, bills like half-baked marlin, the rounded quill with a fluorescent orange head. *Pencil fish*, that's what the old diggers called them, and yes, how we had to pen our stories well to con the bait shops into a sale.

The confusion in the net, fish all crossing each other, locked in panic, bodies woven to create a multitude of silver letters. Many Xs … Ts … Js … Cs, mouths popping, nitrogen-starved Os. How a young summer whiting, tail flared, once looked the perfect Y; an eel, the picture of a feverish S.

We'd pour everything onto the recycled paper surface of Donnybrook's brown sand, the catch a moving paragraph; a funeral notice maybe? Punctuated with the black spots of toadfish, the harpoon of a nervous stingray an exclamation mark, edited before the deadline of a sunset tide …

Mosquito coil,
evenings on the mangroves
boyhood memories

GOLDEN FISH

Sideshow alley explodes! Free-people are paying to be pulverised in aluminium envelopes. Two-dollar snipers are popping down steel ducks in the hope of taking home a hairy monkey.

It's the Brisbane *Ekka!*

We would rush to the Asian Emporium, where for five dollars you were given a hand-net to angle a sea of goldfish in a linoleum-lined façade of an ocean. You caught the poor thing and they put it in a plastic bag with three cups of water held tight with a rubber band.

A one-minute Hemingway for five dollars-worth of sport, and a poor golden fish that wouldn't last the two-hour ride home.

The carnies make a run for you: little demons in the mist of human traffic, their money-mouths and eyes of danger, grifting plenty. This is a gulf stream for sucker fish!

The Brisbane Ekka appears like a jack-rabbit and disappears in the dust of a cold August morning.

But what of the ghosts, of those little lost golden fish?

BOOMERANGS IN A THUNDERSTORM

For Uncle Steve

The clouds are so low that I imagine a puffy hand, reaching out and sending a boomerang off-course. But here we are, like it should be, an uncle and his nephew, throwing boomerangs, tuning the wind. Thunder cracking. Whooping shapes dance across the overcast sky. My lungs are full of the spirits of rain, and it is not long before we are both soaked, riding the storm. Our boomerangs scale the breeze … you should always throw a 'returning' boomerang into the wind … like a sail. On the summit of the sacred owl mountain, *Coot-tha Dreaming,* throwing boomerangs in a thunderstorm.

The unsettled leaf
spirals to a soaked ground,
rain disguised tears

TRASH AND TREASURE

I was up early on Sunday morning, but I felt cleansed; cleaner than if I'd attended Mass. Tomorrow is 'kerbside pick-up'! Firstly, I wheeled out the fuse-exploding dryer, and then its partner-in-crime, the forever-flooding washing machine; they both disappeared within 15 minutes. Killer whitegoods for someone else's laundry. The two futon mattresses laced with rodent faeces from the shed were next; they were snatched up before the rain fell. Our selection of mangled folding chairs had to go; you try to sit in one of those babies and it's a foreseeable vasectomy. And the old lawnmower; a bloke wheeled it away, right out of my hands; that *animal* belonged on a roadside in a warzone where a military demolitions team should have properly disposed of it. Finally, someone stripped the gas barbecue down to its axles – that gem was a suicidal pyromaniac's fantasy on wheels!

This is the part of the Australian Dream that I really love. One Australian collects from another, as an equal, and you may even be considered a neighbour in the classic sense, even though it's reconciliation in deathtraps; but one man's trash is always another's treasure!

BEAUTIFUL BONES

Beautiful bones, beautiful bones
come rest your beautiful bones.

On embrace, feeling your gift of light
where you hold it within
a cage of beautiful bones around your soul,
your soul that should be at rest.
Tired heart beating, travel worn, please share a lullaby with me.

This cage should hold only songlines of love
and poets' musings scripted gently on paper-like wings,
never the death feather of crows.
Silken butterfly dreams and arias of graceful heartstrings
that your love will rest with me a home
beautiful bones, beautiful bones
now come rest your rest your rest your beautiful bones …

THE GIFT OF MEETING GHOSTS

A requiem for Junia

Death drives without brakelights or insurance.

You don't see life so clearly until you run over the loss of a loved one who is so far away.

You try to take the road upon cattle grids where your gait can simply fade away, into the siding of a horrid track. Broken trains push your heart to pieces.

Someone dies so far away and hopefully they will come closer to you, with all that love you have and all the goodness of memory in your heart.

You will see them again.
You will feel them again as dreams permit.

Because only people of shining-want, people like you,
have the gift of meeting ghosts.

THE REMEDY OF BUTTERFLIES

For Tessa

Nothing moves,
the grass has been burnt by frost; almost crisped to a cinder. One would think that nature's cryogenic skin would preserve life. Dawn attempts to revive the scorched earth.

But nothing moves,
first hypothermia, then rigor has set in. Cold spectres muse the wind into subtle whistles, and the chill speaks volumes. Counter-striking slivers of sunshine finally spray-tan this suburban wasteland.

But nothing moves,
not ants, not vermin, nor even the rabble of crows, to paint somewhere beyond the telephone poles a din of afflicted feathers. The early birds have fled; brain-clocks wrestle to inertia-song.

Something moves,
as if the mouth of a new day has yawned, two yellow sulphurs playfully engage one another on the wake of morning breath. Flapping gently, zero velocity to their advantage. Life sparks from tiny wings;
the remedy of butterflies …

WHEN MY POLAROIDS BEGIN TO FADE

For Wim Wenders

I remember a salacious thought one morning, *(or is this a recollection of a salacious morning of thoughts?)* looking into the porcelain hue of her celadon eyes. When the heart turns sour, the camera of the soul takes some of the most horrific images of its journey.

Looking back on my journey through a viewfinder, *(or is this a reflection through a viewfinder of a journey looking backwards?)* looking through the résumé that my conscience keeps of miscalculated risks and positions in which I failed to shine, or even a minute blink of lustre. I shot those opportunities in terrible focus.

I once filmed an entire day of community survival, *(or was this an assumption that the survival of my community would only come through film?)* selfishly looking into the renovation of my mind's scriptorium. I caught things that cannot be recaptured. I should have delved harder into the process of living dreams … then someone wiped the entire day's filming when the camera was formatted.

There are memories of poorly conceived tenets of love, *(or is this recreational plot-development of 'come what may'? No … they were ill-conceived plots of self-preservation!)* looking past the malaise of a lover's tongue and lust for *gloire*. Mist derides images aplenty, and polaroids begin to fade. Salacious is the celadon hue of her, turning to a sepia-toned-folio of engrams.

Does memory liaise with death or mistresses?
                    How chimerical a camera can become.
You feed memories to fuel a malaise,
          when memory is the only medication needed.
Take as prescribed,
          and please, please call me in the morning before I
begin to fade …

FLOTSAM + JETSAM BLUES

For Leah

Goin' to string me a guitar
from the discarded veins of fishermen,
filament tuned in a drift of uncertainty,
I'm goin' to tangle that fishing line free.
                    I'll sweetly ask the sea to sing
                    I'll sing the sea sweetly
                    so the tide can turn for me,
                              I want the tide to turn for me.

They attempted to strangle the water
with this fishing line,
they tried to harvest the silver tears of the sea
and now I'm goin' to string me a guitar
with the jetsam of fishermen,
a flotsam of blues washes over me,
          a flotsam of blues washes over me.

POETRY ON THE GREEN BRIDGE

On the transom of ghosts

(An interactive poem for the commuter)
On this transom, the river's dawning skin … stand
here … *give your breath to the fleeting mist …* stand
here … *in the crimson shadow of Coot-tha's dusk …* stand
here … *and whisper upon night's canvas, whirlpool eyes, the songlines of Kurilpa ghosts …*

Dreaming river triptych

Never the same this river – archaic vein, snaking through the land's dreaming cortex –
submerging provinces; the past, present and future – an aquarelle triptych cultured on every tide …

FINN

We are all watermarked without signs of a recession,
the river lurks in the shadows of our apocalyptic horizons,
buffed; an inverted mushroom cloud.
No one knows the limits of excess it may break;
the *Mark Twain* in nature's aspiration to see its muse
reach full potential.
Even masked as a scourge and scoundrel
no one saw it coming.
And in the aftermath we build rafts
of hope and endearment
borne upon spiritual tides,
strangers become entwined, gilded allies,
however the brim of our narcissism was turned yesterday,
Hey neighbour … I'll be your Huckleberry!

Naïve as we had been, this river is no longer a vent
of childhood adventure.
In a flash we have all relinquished association.
It has been known as *Miramar* and *Brisbane* and Lord knows
any other alias in these days of terror and suspicion.
Albeit, dark and shady this character, we all fell under its spell.
The *Mark Twain* of what lies underneath
is cold and calculative,
but not cut-and-dried.
This is not the same river as yesterday.
To be forensic now serves as a placebo,
like a boomerang in a thunderstorm.
In the ebb, are any of us guilty by association?
Step off the shore, I'll be your alibi … if you be my Huckleberry?

This is a floating world, nothing as anchored as it seems;
a written guarantee is a design flaw on a papier-mâché façade,
job security a mirage in a festering workers' paradise,
while *insurance* has become a dirty curse word.
In the river's wake, how charmed some of our lives have become.
Tomorrow the tide will shed another serpentine identity.
Some will reflect the river's baptismal flair,
many will condemn the water's blatant recidivism;
a bottomless *Mark Twain* of an estuarine underbelly.
And although the *Mark Twain* should cleanse,
on those seductive curves others will bend,
a wash framed in an afternoon of golden light,
on the purple lips of jacaranda blossoms,
marauding and lurid whispers will conspire and beckon:
Join my flotsam heart … come be my Huckleberry.

LET'S TALK!

For Uncle Tiga

'… just because you cannot fight every evil does not mean you should fight no evils.'

– Dennis Prager

Fires burn from voices long-worn of warfare that is unjust, amorphously changing its callous rules of engagement; these nightmares that grow from the veins of our attackers, and from within ourselves.

Let's talk about the daily ruse and hollow conventions of peace that are easily, conveniently broken. A white child dies and a court cries for blood; 100 black children die and the *culpable* call it an accident.

Let's talk like broken records about the state of records broken on this land. Data on our skin alone fills more anthropological library space than any other culture in the world, and yet, we are still misunderstood and being studied?

Fires burn from voices long-worn on the only certainty that Dreaming-wings are clay pigeons for nothing other than brutal hunger. Our enemy cannot hurt us if we have both of our arms wrapped around them in a loving embrace, but it's hard to do that, when they think the black of our skin will rub off onto theirs. The *blackness* is not of our skin, *brother*, but the charcoal of fires where our dreams are cremated.

No one will win this war on succession and replicated acts of gutless valour. After the first stone was thrown, bombs were dropped and hostages were taken. It's that simple!

But, *Let's talk about drafting a treaty … let's talk!*

Let's talk a genocidal monster to sleep; senseless unto its own demise in peaceful dreams … let's talk!

Let's talk reconciliation until we're all too exhausted and the only imperative to take a stand together is to hold each other up and find the comfort of embracement … let's talk!

Let's talk evil into sensual goodness; speak over the red-taped triggers that wait silent and deadly, so they will aim only into the crosshair of an eternal ceasefire … let's talk!

We cannot fight every evil, but as long as a dialogue and even a daily diatribe exists on the destructive principle of evils, *let's just talk!*

Let's talk, until Evil bows to listen,
and the fires burning from voices, that are long-worn, can settle into the beautiful warmth of embers.

And even then when we're done,
let's never stop talking …

MULBERRY STAIN MY MEMORY

We're in Granny Watson's home on Annerley Road and a static kind of excitement is in the air collaborating with a cocktail of tear gas and angst. One hundred metres from the front door three men have scaled onto the roof of Boggo Road Gaol; apparently they were looking for humanity?

I've met some of the men since then who were a part of those riots. There were criminals in that place and a few monsters, but what I know now and what I knew back then is an entirely different story. Many of the chaps in that gaol were only guilty of not conforming to institutional abuse.

Granny Watson sat in her chair while we played cars. Granny's 'eyes' went out scouting like kite-wings in the winds of waiting disaster; the police, the media and the alumni of Queensland's bureaucratic filth sat across the road, stirring the pot of horrors.

Granny Watson grabbed her walking stick and slammed the door shut!

'Have you kids seen my mulberry tree?'

Have you seen my mulberry tree?
Have you seen my mulberry tree?
Tear gas and mulberry stain my memory …

II. NO STANDING ANYTIME

FIGHT CLUB 0.2 (WELCOME TO QUEENSLAND)

The sign greets visitors every hour, erected on the crest, into the valley of our honourable ancestors' spiritual wounds.

> WELCOME TO QUEENSLAND!
> THE 1ST RULE OF QUEENSLAND IS:
> YOU CANNOT TALK ABOUT QUEENSLAND.
> THE 2ND RULE OF QUEENSLAND IS:
> YOU CANNOT TALK ABOUT QUEENSLAND.
> THE 3RD RULE OF QUEENSLAND IS:
> IF YOU'RE NOT WHITE IN QUEENSLAND
> YOU HAVE NO RIGHTS.
> AND THE 4TH AND FINAL RULE OF QUEENSLAND IS:
> IF THIS IS THE FIRST BREATH YOU TAKE IN QUEENSLAND,
> THEN YOU HAVE TO FIGHT!
> POPULATION: 4,676,395 AND COUNTING.

GOD SAVE THE QUEEN! GOD SAVE THE QUEEN! Save the wealth in this playground dystopia for killers, pirates and playboys. This is where the orphans of unofficial wars and police actions are euthanised.

Construction-crane necromancers seed the Mother Earth with the metallic crops of the New World Order. Harvest after harvest, profit after profit, the share market will never crash, when the Dreaming of our country keeps the multinationals afloat in paradise. The blood sport on our sacred sites attracts the world's players.

WELCOME TO QUEENSLAND!
DRIVE SAFELY!
VAYA CON DIOS!

SHOOTING STARS

Slumbering under the moonlight hotel in Barcaldine. Our wine was a good vintage but our showers stunk of rotten egg, so I opted for the campfire. Comets danced above us; a swan lake of astronomical proportions that we could witness from our swags. The choreography was simply stunning, like god herself was pin-pricking the dark shroud of Dreaming while the dance steps of alien-fireflies teased the gaping mouths of black holes that are insatiable, yearning for infinite encore. Light-year flares tangle in the lace of bracken shrubs and emu feathers.

Shooting star fading
from light years of memory,
campfire burns bright

EL DIABLO HIGHWAY

El Diablo Highway is not a songline like those trails of yesterday, before the land's fabric was restitched with veins both barbed and trip-wired.

You are only permitted to travel one way and never against the popular flow. Every journey is fraught with eminent road rage and fatality, El Diablo's horns nailing the innocent. Police stop you by any means necessary and test you for alcohol or drugs when they should be testing for greed and corruption.

Government-funded asylums and prisons are constructed on every shoulder but the powerful are paid to stay out of jail. And what use are they to El Diablo anyway, when they have no souls?

El Diablo Highway keeps the fringes of society curbed and humanity gridlocked. Pits of eternal damnation flame and crackle and there is the ever-present cologne of sulphur; burning tyres linger.

Hitchhikers and the hungry feed on road kill, and luxury cars don't stop for anybody in need until they make the safe city-limits of a mirage that mimics Wall Street. Young people are molested and murdered in front of witnesses who are so concerned with their own affairs that they haven't the capability to report their evidence.

No one should ever come to a full-halt on this stretch; feign car-jacking and make a deal on a crossroad. Whether you're a driver or passenger on El Diablo Highway, it's better the devil you know and always the devil inside.

Reckless vagabond,
a demon's curve in the road,
temptation awaits

THE WHISPERING LANDS

i.

Cruising almost blind into Longreach, we left the protection of the road train's jet stream and drove for our lives. After ten hours on the road, the sun slid down out of sight, remnants of bloodstained horizon danced on the bitumen ahead like St Elmo's fire. Or was it just fatigue playing with my eyes? These whispering lands collaborated with the whispers in the car from weary gravel-strung mouths: *100 klicks to Longreach, we'll be there soon, we'll be there soon …* Our mobile phones croaked and died, 'cause you can't get a signal out here – the lines diverted to Canberra, where politicians gamble on the profits from the sale of Telstra, while the people of this country continue to live but can't be heard.

ii.

As the last shards of light disappear in the west, whispers in this land become more apparent; especially from the mouths of road kill, death-wrapped in agony, and then the loudest whispers of them all … grey-shapes that jack-rabbit from the mesquite brush. How the darkness softens the hide of mulga and the quiet song of kangaroo.

Come collide with me, let's collide, let's collide away …

The dry tongues of this land echo through the winter, and into a drought-blown summer of a neo-discontent.

ROAD FIRE

For Alesa – set on Mununjali country, late spring 2013

Sun has risen over the ridges
for several hours now
and before the highway
an incendiary wave appears
where heat-haze will soon stake
its working ghosts.

A mature red-belly-black serpent
animates the bitumen before us.
A good 1.5 metres in body
scarlet belly, massaging path,
lighting the road.

Of my mind's eye
I easily forget
how venom is always ahead.
Dark and deadly and precious and ignored.
Until you are awakened on country
you are reminded of how important it is
that some paths need to be crossed.

CYCLONE CITY

We'd just laid a dear uncle to rest and I was still in my funeral swagger; black on black. I travelled from Sydney to Brisbane, and then Brisbane to Darwin, via Sydney back-step shuffle, in a fortnight of memories painted only in a palette of blues. I'd never been to Darwin before, but I knew enough to know this country. My nana was awarded an Order of Australia for helping in the big clean-up when our people up here had *nothing* and then Tracy took that away from them too. As kids we lay on the front room floor at night as a scarlet lamp bathed our imagery; ghost stories of how clever-men in the Gulf can dance and sing a vengeful wind! And now I was here, in a black suit, the cabin cracks open and we almost spill out like yolks. Instantly, the heat bones you; *sticky old man fingers on your body* ... just like the way you don't want to be touched! I felt like a dishcloth by the time I completed my first gig, a cruise on Darwin Harbour, opening for Neil Murray. I kept one eye on my page and another on any passage of crocodile lines in the night water. When the gig was over, Neil and I went back to the air-conditioned sanctum of the hotel and he wired musings of Warumpi tales into the wee hours. It was pure rock 'n' roll! I only had a dream's-sleep before jumping into a booth on Darwin's ABC desk for a live-on-air chat with my favourite percussionist, Rob Hirst. A day in the eye of this storm then, before I was on a panel with Frank Moorhouse: '*Martinis with Moorhouse*'. The tropical dusk simmered our poison while we rattled the audience with husky throats; Frank reminiscing bygone days in New York's Algonquin Hotel. I had no recollection by then of my contribution? Tepid martinis were fed to us, and my eyes rolled into the Arafura sunset.

Back on a jet a couple of hours later, like I'd been slung on a *Shanghai-belt*, still dressed in black, but everyone in Darwin sweats anyway, and before I could turn off my phone, a message slaps me up the side of the head … a journalist that was with me the night before was hit by a car and is now recuperating in a Darwin hospital. Poor *fulla*! Would have been safer maybe, if he'd rocked the kasbah in Baghdad instead of Darwin, as is the want of many journalists in these days when writing the fortunes of terror can make you a celebrity.

But please, *please*, *PLEASE* skip the emergency procedures and *fly me to the moon*, before I'm carried away forever, in this cyclone city!

BLACKTRACKER ... BLACKWRITER ... BLACKSUBJECT

Sometimes, when I pick up a pen, I'm the *blacktracker*; following an ink-trail across a page of country, to find lost and wayward words. And then sometimes, when the grasp on the pen is very good, I'm the *blackwriter*; the *blackwriter* who can sense the resentment from other *blacksubjects* who have been denied the Queen's diction. With or without the pen though, I'm always the *blacksubject*; the *blacksubject* scouting out upon an endless trail of the Queen's death-notes. Propaganda and poison ink; the medicine the Queen's children now use to edit *blacksubjects*. Occasionally, I'm the *blacksubject*, *blackwriter* and *blacktracker,* and we all ride out together. The Queen pays the *blacktracker* for some of my dirty work, the *blackwriter* feeds my Dreaming to the Queen's tongue, and then *blacksubjects* don't come to my poetry readings, thus, I pay for my words. Alienated only as the *blacksubject.* But with or without the pen, it's the *blacksubject* who will inherit the earth. Because at the end of the day, the *blacksubject* can't be bought like the *blacktracker,* and the *blacksubject* can't be seduced like the *blackwriter,* 'cause the *blacksubject* will always know ... it's with the pen that the lies are used to overwrite the Dreaming, and the written word will never be worth the country it's written on.

PARALLEL OZ

It's the Lucky Country's closet; a dark interior with frontier skeletons. Whirly-winds run rampant, spawning red-sand mandalas of chaos. These frenetic twisters find easy prey on ochre-kissed Dorothys, carrying them off to Parallel Oz. In Parallel Oz, neither the good witches or the wicked afford these Dorothys little pairs of magic red shoes … *there's no place like a broken home … there's no place like a broken home … there's no place like a broken home.* The yellow-brick road is pock-marked with massacre sites and the Wizard, the Wizard of Parallel Oz; he holds Dorothy hostage to a mutual obligation agreement. The Straw-man has the grazing monopoly, the Tin-man has the mines, and the Lion waits in the spinifex with the long-grass drinkers. Parallel Oz and its rag-doll Dorothys; not just an Advance Australia Fair*ytale*, but a reality spinning out of control, gaining catastrophic momentum.

INTERVENTION ANGELS

For the 'guardian' Angels of Tennant Creek

In Tennant Creek, the kids had a nocturnal game they played called '*Jealous-ing*'; where a group of young women would mimic the role of sirens and croon a group of young men, trying to lure them out into the sleeping, desert-washed streets.

One of the young tribes was known as the 'Angels', but some of their members tagged 'Angles' all over the south side of town. A teacher pleaded with me, *If you wanna do any good while you're here, teach them the difference between the words A N G E L S and A N G L E S … it's bloody embarrassing!*

A lot of the public servants I met thought it was that easy in Tennant Creek too. You simply take an 'Angle' tagged onto a wall and turn it into an 'Angel'; silence its country and clip its wings, as an impending government intervention looms …

like a sandstorm, I never saw it coming either

Just as easy to fix a curved piece of wood into these angels' hands and land a boomerang on the moon …

On a desert night,
sullen Angels are singing,
calling all Angels

STRANGE FISH

Alice Springs, winter 2006

An abandoned school of silver shapes, partially imbedded in the sandy skin of the Todd River. These strange fish seemed to have perished in a pack, almost like lemmings, when the river disappeared into the dreaming of evaporation. Back in the city we know these strange fish by urban-zoological nomenclature:

Goonius baggas.

Vessels for cheap wine, the most distinguishing feature, a white bulbous plastic eye, like a Cyclops. But here on the Todd these eyes are permanently fixed on the desert sun. Eyes that once held magic! Eyes that were once the gateways of inebriated souls, and now their souls are bled too; shiny bodies, awaiting fossilisation. Suspended in animation; a sad reflection of a past tide, caught in the immortal sands of this winding, broken hourglass.

XERODERMA

For Sandra Thibodeaux

We stopped on the road to Uluru … the rock just sat in her place and didn't seem to come any closer for hours.

We walked over a spinifex beach and waded upon the salt of Lake Amadeus … I've never seen anything more magic. Salt kills the devil's stride … I found all sorts of hooved tracks that stopped before the frozen edge of the desert.

A.D. Hope penned an Australia of 'immense stupidity'.
A viral Hope was burned out here
and I can see why
he chose to write about this landscape as he rejected it
and it rejected him.

The spinifex is beautiful and the mirage could possibly carry ghosts beyond our reckoning.

That is why the old people trapped demons here.

I could have stayed here forever and been a gatekeeper, comfortable on the watch of furies trapped in this salty hourglass.

But Uluru wasn't getting any closer on the sun's evening,
desert breeze
kissing whiskers of this xeroderma.

INSOMNIA

Overlooking Gladstone
from my hotel balcony
                                        perched
                                                      like a gargoyle
the lights of a ship drift by
and I think I think of fireflies
                                        because
I hear nothing but the constant buzzing of industry
                                        in the salt-filled air
the silica-night-ripple of the toxic harbour
and although prone
to insomnia, self-loathing and homesickness,
                                                      I feel quite comfortable

                                        in this city that can't seem to sleep.

A POSTCARD FROM YARRABAH

Artist statement on the experience of the ABC mini-series Bush Slam *hosted by H.G. Nelson – one town, two poets, three days to write a poem.*

Yarrabah is like any other Aboriginal mission. It was founded on brutality and that brutality is still deeply ingrained in every aspect of life in the present, whether it's dealt out now by the local, state or federal bureaucracies who control the destinies of Yarrabah's people. 'Yarri' is a beautiful place, but I immediately recognised its dislocation from Cairns. In many Murri communities you'll hear people describe their remoteness as a state of being, 'out of mind and out of sight', and from the lavish tourist mecca of Cairns, Yarrabah definitely exists in this state … and that's where I fell down as a raconteur, because there were just too many stories and testaments that needed to be told and there just wasn't enough time to write.

I saw the names of my forebears in the 'mission-log' in Yarrabah's library … my name was there; and it's the name my son proudly bears. My great-grandfather and all the children of his generation were born into slavery and their being established places like Yarrabah … there's no myths in these stories … there's no romance, and I wish I just could have composed myself better than I did. I loved working with Kate, H.G. and the crew … I loved everyone in Yarrabah … I was just the wrong person for this job … Yarrabah is struggling in its survival, and I just can't shake the feeling that I was some kind of hollow literary voyeur on a three-day visa …

elusive
Yarrabah's beautiful community
unfolded right in front of me,
but their stories ever-elusive
like the wreck in front of the church
and how its resident crocodile remained a mystery to me,
but maybe after three days
I'm still city-blind and blocked-up,
and can't see for lookin'?
But I can hear the squawking sea-hawk … Guyulla,
shadows the tidal wake,
echoes off the mountains,
beautiful Yarrabah song …

Kate refers to Kate Fagan, poet and folk musician, who participated in the poetry slam.

POSTCARDS FROM THE LOCK-UP

What's in a name?

Inside here, my prison number is 1788, followed by my ABN, followed by 1967, the year of the referendum, when black people won their citizenship in this country. When I was working in the Territory recently, the 'old' people instructed me to call the dead 'Kumanjai' … so maybe that's what I should call myself? My name here in the lock-up is 1788, followed by my ABN, followed by 1967. No one in the *writing game* pronounces or understands my middle name anyway … so I wouldn't mind being called Kumanjai, confined in this space where all the other inmates are ghosts.

Incident report

It was Sunday, 4.35am, but I was already awake when the sharp brutal blast happened. It was followed closely by glass tap dancing across the alleyway below my cell block. There were no voices; just another mute assassin in audible shadows.

I'm not a dog! I didn't see anything! You can't make me grass!

The next morning I discovered that someone had wrapped a vodka bottle around the lock-up's heavy iron gate. And however secure I was within the walls, the perpetrator of this assault was loose on the streets of general-population … a dangerous prisoner of the Newcastle night.

STEALING KISSES

Advice to emerging poets

I'm in this 'lock-up'; my only crime to date is a bit of bad writing. Being a writer today is like being a burglar anyway. The mind of a reader and the collective conscious of any audience can be as hard to crack, away from mass media, as the door of a titanium safe. To open the mind of a reader, one must deploy the stealth of particular words and character. When you're a poet, it's a little bit harder. Poets don't often receive the same welcoming as accomplished novelists, so quite often a poet must work off the fence of a cold audience. Of course, if you have a 'thief's touch' with the pen, you'll easily crack the combination of any individual's captivation without the alarm of their insecurities going off. Sometimes this will happen without an audience even realising they've been taken; you've been stealing their kisses all along.

WHAT IS WRONG WITH THIS PICTURE?

In response to Charles Blackman's painting The Student

Prognosis

The last time she was seen, a ribbon ran through her hair like a varicose vein, painful in its brevity, crowned her greening image upon flashlight hollow eyes. She was clasping a book of unknown content, through a thick, forested crowd. Witnesses under wide-brimmed hats, too preoccupied … gaunt she may have been, fragile she was, maybe in the throes of consumption of darkness? No one saw anything, lest the dark light that they traversed and possibilities, having severed any of their umbilicals that can cause a major haemorrhage to the *not knowing …*

Diagnosis

The last time she was seen, pain began in the sinister lining of the formidable crowd. Her nexus – the umbilical between parent and child – the line of sight, was severed indefinitely, followed by paralysis due to entropy inflicting the region of her departure, the neural solidifying of fact to fiction, placement to prodigal. An equation became of the poppet, a tiny tumour that fills an infinite void.

Placebo

What is wrong with this picture? Artists should avoid the surgical procedure of epitaph … our paints are merely bandaids over a gaping nightmare … there are very few cures.

DEAFENING COLD

As the plane made approach, I whispered an acknowledgement; my respect to the Kulin peoples, upon whose country I'd be landing. There are songlines here that sing as loud as the day the tramlines ripped through the Dreaming … but those tramlines can't sing … *those tramlines can't sing.*

Walking across Swanston Street, blowing my 'D' harpoon into the crisp air, unnoticed, unmolested, I played freely in Melbourne's Friday night chaos …

the tram-song
ain't louder
than the train-song,
but lower even
is the taxi-song …

on a Flinders Street crossroad
hundreds of cabbies
stop the traffic
with their blues;
the city just rolls over
and yawns …

a cab-driver ain't goin' home tonight,
and won't be going home ever …

The Kulin peoples are the traditional owners of Melbourne.

NAPALM KEROUAC AND THE MADDENING NIGHT

'The bonfire shared =
the yearning factotum, international dandy,
spate of the charming flare.'
– Corey Wakeling, 'The Tar Fires'

My aunty Jenny turns to me between two conversations, in which she is an authority of all the matters at hand.

Eh, nephew, this place used to be a mental institution … there's a lot of ghosts here!

And that seemed right on the money, because poets are the maddest creed of writer, and quite often the unaccounted ghosts of the literary world. But, I'd rather sit with and listen to the lungs of a sensitive, anxious writer as they count each syllable of their life. A brash writer will consider their motives sane, whilst flaunting the wealth of a three-book deal and not even realising they've actually signed on a dotted line, which could eventually drive them crazy!

A young Turk takes the microphone and with a wink and a smile he reads a poem written by my Mununjali Uncle, Lionel Fogarty. He begins by telling us all he's a 'bit' nervous, but *HE* has *IT!* I can safely assume that he must also write as forensically as he interprets the travels of another writer's shoes.

The rain is falling and the darkness extends cold fingers. The lights of Balmain Road are pulled back from the writers centre as if light itself were an editor, crossing us all out. But this young Kerouac simply napalms the air with the fire of Uncle Lionel's words, pressure-cooking the spectral air of the maddening night.

Burn, baby, burn!

TOO MANY SECRETS

Wagga Wagga, winter 2000

I can't sleep here, on this Wiradjuri land; upon this hill of learning. Awake until the sun comes up and the morose voices subside; the dawn light blades whispers back into the creases of scarred country. I can't sleep here, in the writers centre; a beautiful place with so many bright voices that burn into the night, spectral sages cloud my ears like moths to a flame. Too many secrets here; ceremony ground now a university. There is too much information in this place here, singed, black pages that the granite boulders relay in monolithic volumes. Tumbleweeds spin and stutter. The air licks with a cold wet mouth that bears the driest parables … I just can't sleep on this beautiful soil that was sung … and sewn with too many secrets … even by the daylight hours, in the peppered corners of the cottage, tirades in session and ghosts forging motions. Outside, vicious birds swoop across the battlefield, picking at the skins of audible shadows …

Dark fruit on the tree
one, two, three, four, five and six
seven crows singing

PATH-FINDING

i.

(An axiom from Woodford, circa 2005)
Two eagles circled above grass dancing, with feathers of the
  wedge-tailed
when an elder advised her, that it was a sign of love without fail,
and in a matter of hours, confessions and embrace
a knoll on Jinibara skin we discovered a solitary place.
    (Her blood hailed from Finland …)
With every sultry kiss I asked the country to heed,
Please old fullas let me love … and please let me beloved?

ii.

(Norway, 72 hours later …)
An eagle awoke me as our car followed the fjord into Riddu Riđđu. The majesty of its span was an incendiary sight, even in these freezing environs. My publisher and brother, Anders, pointed to a break in the mountain range on our southern flank: *That's Finland over there, where your lady is from!* The eagle swept the fjord and left us, and it was on the same stretch, we countered a sullen crossroad where the great Sami poet Áillohaš made his way to the Dreamtime.

And the eagle; like the midnight sun, made unscheduled, spectral appearances to take us in.

TEARS RUNNING ABOVE ZERO

For Anders

Winter may be on hiatus for a brief spell; yet, here and there the Arctic sun has still to undress the landscape from some lingering belts of snow. We've left Kåfjord, heading north to Alta, for some of the best sea-trout streams in the world. Our guide, Bjørn (the Bear), is on leave from the Norwegian Coast Guard. He spends most of his year patrolling the headwaters of Hemingway's Gulf Stream. His Audi station wagon has three drink holders for every passenger, and each is stocked with tall cans of dark Scandinavian pilsener. The temperature rises to nine degrees, so it's warm enough for a *brewski* at 3am … The glare of the midnight sun paints the landscape a palette that could possibly remind me of back-home right now; an autumn Sunday morning, 11am on an overcast day in Brisbane … but I'm on the other side of the world and at home all those dear to me are sleeping.

The mountains here weep! They welcome the temporary warmth. Cascades fall from their summits and the green stubble of winter's coma grows on their faces. These mountains were made in the last ice age; they're not like the rough igneous-plugs back at home. They are smooth, with inclines that resemble enormous skateboard ramps. We listen to David Bowie's 'Changes' and discuss Hemingway's short story, 'Now I Lay Me', because we'll have to dig for worms, if perchance, this morning's frost hasn't thwarted us? Here and there, pockmarks like braille tell the stories of German soldiers who hid in these mountains, as the Resistance, Norge and Finn sharpshooters picked them off. The snipers draped in white, behind opaque armoured plates on the rises, taking aim in front of midday's snow-blinding grin.

This is not a bleak landscape now, just one of rejuvenation. The German blood that shares my veins reminds me that I need to pay further respects to this country. We stop for a stretch and the fleeting ghosts of winter are like a vortex from our Cheshire-grins. The fish are waiting in a river not far away … just a few more fjords to negotiate and the occasional pet reindeer that hinders our entry onto its turf.

A roadside stream filters the mountain's want to commune with its steps, and I drink from this pure nectar, like I am taking Mass in a sacred place, the mountain's tears running above zero …

Norwegian spring,
crying softly the mountains,
tundra catching tears

THE MOUNTAIN, THE MONUMENTS AND THE MAN …

Yogyakarta, winter 2006 – As part of the Utan Kayu Literary Biennale, we embarked on a roadtrip through Java and made pilgrimage to several of the Candi (lava-stone temples). Uncle Goenawan Mohamad – sage, poet, journalist – explained that in the thick of fighting during the Indonesian National Revolution (1945–49), a lone soldier guarded Candi Prambanan temple. Although having no weapons and few provisions, he refused to abandon his post for the duration of the entire conflict, when Indonesia won independence from the colonial oppression of the Dutch …

To the west, the skyline illustrates a rumbling palsy of emphysematous cloud; this is the breath of Merapi, the Fire Mountain. This young Turk of a volcano has a lethargic body, stomach reflux, anger-management issues, holding the archipelago to ransom. Merapi's rapacity seems insatiable!

The majestic lava-stone points of Candi Prambanan are just thin needles with Merapi simmering in their midst. This Hindu shrine was erected in honour of Trimūrti; a creator Brahmā of preservation and destruction.

[I can do you, reader, little service in being able to encompass textually the architectural enigma of this 9th-century achievement … or the immensity of the Fire Mountain's girth!]

Spiderwebs of bamboo scaffold surround the grey towers after the last time Merapi threw his weight around and the temple walls were partially desecrated in a moment of seismic madness. Now the landscape looks like a building block playground of the gods, sedentary monoliths waiting to be reassigned.

Fire Mountain is a juvenile; he revels in his power, flirts with the ambivalence of nature, abuses his might, and will inspire and command love poems and death threats. He lives with his head in the clouds, like many adolescents.

Trimūrti shrines are but ancient mariners who have navigated a millennial wash in spiritual winds. They have witnessed several epochs of religions. Reverently though, one cannot perceive these tributes as ruins; they are merely vacant. In the equatorial heat-haze few ghosts dance, as if they have been evacuated until their home is deemed fit to be safely repossessed.

There is almost a spectral feeling of calm here. Maybe the spirit of the solitary guard remains on watch over the temples? Uncommon valour in death as in life, the soul of an isolated, unarmed Javanese warrior. A selfless man, with the one characteristic that the awesome firepower of a volcano could never portray: an unquestionable love for country.

HEART OF DARKNESS

For Sean Whelan

How the Javanese jungle pulses in wait, like an enormous arachnoid that needs no introduction. It is dark and deadly. Bats make the atmosphere swell, carrying clouds on their heavy flaps, black fans that do nothing to quell the equator's breath.

We sit at the base of Borobudur temple, a lava-stone monolith in praise of Buddha … 504 statues and 2672 relief-panels carved in servitude of Buddha … stone shaped from flesh that yearned enlightenment.

A Melbourne poet takes the podium and paints a macabre portrait of the day that the sombre but beautiful troubadour Elliott Smith stabbed himself in the heart!

Bats pepper the sky and the audience is gobsmacked by the reading. We are suddenly all vassals of the jungle; *this heart of darkness.* The dim beauty of the Indonesian night, to celebrate a life vanquished. How the mouths of lovers can be burnt in the heat of the moment and hearts tainted of impotent darkness.

The solemn words of a poet, enshrined at the steps of Borobudur temple, in honour of the fateful karma of Elliott Smith … *the horror … the horror!*

WHEN PENCILS SING EXCUSES

For Madonna

A MESSAGE TO MY PUBLISHER: I'm sorry you haven't seen or heard from me; I've been lost in a good poem, I've been travelling with a dictionary of freaks, I've been teaching pencils to sing … A MESSAGE TO MY PUBLISHER: A message in a bottle, dictated from bottles, trying to muse a Tom Waits three-day growth and growl *and I'd rather have a bottle in front of me than a frontal lobotomy … Ahhhh!* I'm sorry I haven't called, I'm sorry I didn't write you a note, I'm sorry I didn't write you that manuscript that's five years in the making and I've got enough excuses to fill five manuscripts … I've been scribbling excuses just like poems just like excuses just like rectums and everyone has a rectum, has excuses, has poems coming out of their rectums, and every rectum is a critic! The dog ate my manuscript. My granny died … again. *Ahhhh!* A MESSAGE TO MY PUBLISHER: I've been lost in a good poem, I've been travelling with a dictionary of freaks, I've been teaching pencils to sing, I've been filing excuses in bottles, bottles been filling me with messages, *PLEASE, CALL YOUR PUBLISHER …* 'Cause I need to find myself from inside that good poem. I need to stop showcasing a dictionary of freaks. And I need to switch off the muse, inside the sweet voices of pencils …

THE NIGHT WE LOST CHARLES BUKOWSKI'S VOICE

It was a dark and stormy night of clichés. The rain coming down, drowning the shadows, and my motley crew, well, that hotel room just couldn't hold us. We threw everything into a black sports bag – cigarettes, hotel stationery, little shampoo sachets, an expensive bottle of malt whisky and a cassette of Charles Bukowski reading his poetry at UCLA – off we went into the dampness of the streets, looking for a party. It all went pear-shaped though, in a cab on George Street … we witnessed *the filth* chasing a black man I knew … we ushered him into the cab, only to be surrounded by imposing uniforms as the windows of the vehicle grew foggy, like a greenhouse effect; the winter of our discontent.

Is this how a goldfish views our world?

Anyway, the cabby *hated coppers!* he said, flew through traffic and a red light … and that blackfulla, he jumped us all eventually, owing the $20 he pledged to ferry us across the river Styx of our evening … how black the night looked when that taxi driver cut us loose … we death-marched back into town, and with our last few dollars howled vodka, deep throat echoes into shot glasses … but the bartender could smell the whisky in the bag … we didn't screw the lid on tight enough! He quickly asked us to leave; the ol' 86er! Whisky leaking all over the Charles Bukowski cassette and drowning his voice forever … *how ironic!*

I eventually had to crawl home through the soppy train yards and weeds … falling into an open sewer, ripping my shirt on bits of exposed metal shards … stared up at the lights of the city and smiled, thirsty … thirsty … thirsty …

Empty vodka glass
in the 3am city
alley cat meow!

III. NO NAKED FLAMES

BOMBING OUT

Winter 2000

It was standing room only in West End Library; poetry punters and the Queensland Police Bomb Squad. I was the third poet in a week to receive a death threat – at least someone seemed to be reading our work, rather than ignoring it. The vibe actually helped in my reading and an untapped energy surfaced, the likes I hadn't felt before … I even sold a book to a brunette cop who stayed around. Not bad for an emerging poet who needed a sympathetic audience, free publicity and a buzz to carry me through the hour,

without the chance of bombing out …

LOVE POEM

He had L O V E tattooed across his clenched right fist, followed by P O E M, etched in a vagabond's quill, across the other. And with these fists coming at you in unison, you copped a taste of his, LOVE POEM. He walked the crooked lines of this world, straightening them out with a little, LOVE POEM. 'My old man fixed the world with his fists … in his memory I have a little, LOVE POEM …' He'd start out with the POEM and then he'd flourish it with some LOVE, his one-two, two-one strategies with bloody tattooed gloves. He no longer used his real name, just the combination of slugs, LOVE POEM, LOVE POEM, POEM, LOVE, LOVE POEM, LOVE POEM, POEM, LOVE … this hard, crooked world could use some tenderising, with a little LOVE POEM, LOVE POEM, LOVE … POEM.

THIS WONDERFUL JEZEBEL

The cruellest woman in the world is the one whom I loved the hardest, the sweetest, ally of my heart's fear. She can still twist the knife in my back where she stuck me so good the blade went as far to rattle my cage, carved an abyss and created horribly beautiful scar tissue. In my mind's eye jezebel dances little dervishes like numbing migraines, fucking me with her callous grin, fucking me over like she has always done. And sadly I know I am one of a collection and morbidly I am jealous; I am not her only victim that has been taken for a lark. Telling me she loved me was the best literary fiction she'll ever compose. Such a torturous, sweet muse,

this wonderful jezebel,

I'll always love you …

A WARNING THAT RANG TRUE

For Kelly

She spoke above the polarity of her dancing routine and tried to convince me that love was not a solution; she basically told me every night at 1am that she wanted to buy a farm and it didn't help the relationship when I'd stagger in with a grin at the end of her shift … *I'm here to take you home, baby!* There really was nothing poetic about my diplomacy. I remember her first words of cementing doubt, looking over the Brisbane River at midnight, when the muse of the tide even lusted, competed to be as arousing as her blue eyes, moonlight projecting unwritten love poems upon her deep olive skin. Mosquitos were just as intoxicated as I was, in her wake.

This isn't going to work if you fall in love with me …

STIRRING IN NIGHT

For Heli

I still taste the night with a child's lips, and as you invite me into the dimness of your embrace, I seek the past ghosts who may have claimed this sacred domain behind the perfect curvature of your breasts, waiting for the tricks of the mind's eye to appear.

Though I wander through the valley of the shadow of your flesh, I try to fear no evil. I am scared of the dark. I remember nights when I waited for the floating white sheets of ghosts to appear, and now, as a man, I fear the same brethren of those spectres, the spirits of other people, left in the linen, ghost-tracking them in through the aura of your soothing warmth. Pilot lights, your bedroom eyes scorch the darkness and teach me to breathe, teach me to pace myself, teach me to trust you …

Your loving fingers
dancing the curves of my back,
whispers in the night

THROUGH WINTER'S BREATH ... AND A THANK YOU

For Dee

Birds angle on a winter's breath
cold teardrops into the mouths of the hungry.

Fly close to me
to my heart; to our hearts
the words on winter's wing will carry us.

Hold me close as I will hold your words
no shadows could be found in the wake of these dark wings.

You held me in a vessel and you carried me through a bad
winter's breath … thank you.

PAPER WINGS

For the yellow sulphur

Beauty
folds and unfolds
bathing in the day's warmth
spending all its delicate hours
kissing gently each blooming-flower
nature's gift, wrapped in paper wings
folding and unfolding
rising, falling
beauty.

WARNING

The following work is protected under copyright by the author. It is illegal (and morally corrupt) to sample or appropriate parts of this work or the entirety of this book for creative and commercial gains, or flagrant self-promotion, without the author's permission. Piracy and plagiarism of concepts and writing are not a victimless crimes and affect entire communities of artists.

A falling raindrop
has no shared characteristics with a waterfall;
it cannot call itself a waterfall,
it will only ever be a raindrop.

The bedroom mirror
can only reflect the serene skin of a lake;
a lake is an ephemeral living entity,
and the mirror will remain a dead-pool in the bedroom.

Certain mimic beetles
will often copy venomous spiders;
unaware that they have waded into their own snare,
predator victim to their own prey.

END OF DAYS

Circa 2012

I now study the *Financial Review*, like a conspiracy theorist studies the Mayan calendar; 2012 the End of Days! Headlines like MINING BOOM HOLDS UP ECONOMY just reveal how close we are to losing the Dreamtime. And if the *Financial Review* is right, coal exports will cut the soul out of my elders' Rainbow Serpent. The Australian government will sell uranium to India, and China will invest five trillion dollars into Australian real estate. BUY-SELL-BUY-SELL … BUY … SELL … My bank manager sends me a death threat; I'm 34 cents overdue on my VISA card and some faceless young tie-wearing bastard hammers a big FOR SALE sign in front of my hedge. And then some faceless bastard side-swipes my new car at the local grocery store. Where has my Australian Dream gone? There's nothing as sexy as a crisp dollar … nothing as valuable in these days when the Mayans predicted it would all end. I carry a *Wall Street Journal* under my arm. Wrap me up in it when I die and lay me somewhere cheap … stick my sarcophagus together with cheques that bounce …

a folded dollar
crisp like a butterfly's wings,
living for a day

CLOUD BURST

For T.S. Eliot

Cloud burst, and another sky falls. A blight of sun causes all feather to lose flavour in the wind. But our children will still have their mobile phones and dial the clouds in angst of predator-drones. The crows are gone and broken windows only catch the breath of dying trees. No matter how sorry the horizon, a child's foresight will always wonder of the beauty in a falling sky.

'Look Mumma … a death-bird!'

But Mumma doesn't look at the sky since it has soured. Mumma takes a peg and pins a damp sheet to the flimsy clothes hoist. Mumma counts the kinks in the wire and measures her own lifeline.

'Mumma can't look now, baby,
there may not be any sunlight tomorrow …'

Mumma takes the small child inside their shelter, abandoning the weathered fabric to subtly dance alone; it could be tomorrow's death shroud?

And this is the way the world ends,
and this is the way the world ends,
and this is the way the world ends.
As the clouds quietly burst,
not with bang, but a lethal breeze.

The sky is falling,
ghosts take shelter in shadow
and the air cries foul

FLAME TREES

For Uncle Robert Forster

Jacaranda avenues are being trimmed by the wear of so many artists. What is this endless musing in a comfortable Brisbane season of discontent?

Jacarandas simply don't grow in the postcodes of the poor.

Uncle Grant McLennan was one of the only poets to take the limb of a jacaranda and turn it into a boomerang, *on the streets of our town.*

Unfortunately, the only blue-purple I know of the *Jacaranda mimosifolia* is a botanical memoir of the hate that grew within a woman I loved. She went to the U of Q. She is a firecracker but will never amount to a flame tree.

My purple-heart sits on my brow … you sucker-punched me good, baby!

I recall driving into Kempsey and at my flanks a majestic honour-guard of flame trees saluted, bloody and ripe! These are trees that are synonymous with fighters and battle! Give me a flame tree any day of the week over bloom that bruises memory.

All of the jacarandas in Brisbane are victim of too many writers and extra-sensitive minstrels who rattle the violet-belle. But it's done and dusted and obviously, too late now.

Like floggin' a dead horse purple, with a death rattle.

MURDER OF CROWS

Zulu time: 1824 hours, Friday Night Blues, winter, circa 1992

Cutting slate on a cold morning with the promise of $150 on my cuff; crows gather in a vile breeze and uptake various positions on a telephone wire. *Who are those death-birds calling?* Someone dropped a body bag from a Burger King on the bitumen. In the dictionary of warfare, this could be classed as a 'Passage of Lines'.

The jackhammer hurts but it's cash and I'll stay compliant until the foreman calls it quits and shows me the money. The dark-birds sat on the cable all day and crowed like peacocks; beautiful B-52s in a 'hold' position above the innocent. *What payloads do they carry?* They are soiled envelopes of curses in the wind; wings of an apocalypse grift. Of what mandate should they hang over the heads of workers whilst millionaires are killing themselves softly with the wings of ample tax-brackets?

Black-wings hung there until dusk. Those crows were characters in **bold** on a good, sunset canvas. The job was a near-to-death experience, but worth every cent; hard cash in my mouth.

I carried and dragged, half-shagged, off the bus, into the Camp Hill pub, and a smiling young politician by the name of Kevin Rudd bought me a beer. Sipping the amber brew of his jug and looking out on the ragged night, contemplating the thoughts of my own execution tomorrow, if I'd make it, in another murder of crows.

UNFORGIVEN

I will never forgive myself for telling you
that I loved you
struggling on my knees for a season in hell
little glass skulls dingle in my ears
as the breeze whispers
ectoplasm
from the memory of your salty lips

and when you ended it all
I had no feet to die upon
no throat left to bark like a dog
and nothing of a heart
or a cheek to turn

and yet I'd do it all again

hauling my used honour

just to fall back
into a fallow trough
of your soul's mire

and unforgiving
but I can't stop loving you …

ENERGY

Condensed energy builds momentum and disperses,
sending shards through space and time
like a swarm of meteorites
or breeze through a cherry blossom grove,
the ambivalent resonance of spent energy.

30 MINUTES OF FREEDOM

For Ian Friend

Time is running out and the heartbeat of my liberty could flatline. The cup has *runneth over* and the wine has gone to water. The phone is cut off and wolves are at the door. The dial tone was like a stopwatch that lingered. Rock salt I have spread, across the crow's feet of my gait. There can be no coming back from this hour. I've tallow stored for reflection. Shards of broken mirror I am bound. 15 minutes to ground zero and counting down. The coffee is colder, the traffic outside is louder; a butterfly's life has more credibility. 10 minutes into this break of day. 5 minutes to check emails. I have not accounted for the time I will need to make promises good; penance with pits and pendulums, a raven's feather past, past the butterfly's life in wait. Bondage and mandatory sentences, time for confession: *Where did it go? Was it in waste or words?* As the music stops I am the solitary soul standing, put here on my own accord having wasted the hours. Absentia and deadlines … 30 minutes of freedom.

Wings of desire
an open and shut whisper;
the calm breeze of death

THE RUNNING END … (GHOSTS WON'T COVER ME …)

I've acquired a ream of fine-lines from a 24-hour store and those 100 pages wrapped in cellophane have not made their weight in the last cut of my gold coins. I wanted to compose until midnight, to look at the red beacon on the Green Bridge, again, and again, and again. Sitting at this desk and finding landing-lights over Archerfield of clear running; small wasps in a curtain of star-studded breeze. But I can't believe I'm running this early, out of paper so soon, running on empty, running out of money, confidence and excuses. Yet, someone will always want to publish a poem at the end of next week and a debt collector could be always lurking in the dim cocktail of any day's reckoning. I have to pay up, sometime? They know my bank account and I know theirs. I have positive money some days and in the equilibrium, my negative money spins. I'll throw my coins; heads and tails in that break. I'll just listen for the feather-dust of a magpie's call; a scout-bird of my frail dark skin.

At the dark stretch of this day, three pages short of midnight; running I am. I shouldn't live like this, on a broke-down pen!

I do it because it's what I know. It's not what I'm proud of. I can always make a gamble out of fresh words; a yard of weeds from tomorrow morning's break of day in a mash of crumpled paper.

But that's how I got into this mess in the first place! Ghosts can't cover me now on a credit-check of poorly settled debts. I am on the running end, unless a breeze of dollars blows soon.

With each new play and skim of credit, I'm just making more compartments and closets. They are in their entirety, full of worthless skeletons.

On a death sentence
commanding a wayward quill,
mercenary

VISITING HOURS

Stand back … keep your body and hands away from the bars … the bars, the frets of the instruments that played with the dark … stand back … keep your body and hands away from the bars … bars that chime, forever echo the futility of shadows that move between them, contact with the living prohibited … out of mind, out of sight … shadows whose names will never be cleansed of stain from conviction … and the victims' names soon lost in the incarceration of public memory … stand back … keep your body and hands away from the bars; the frets of the instruments that played with the dark … the lost band who once strummed a chord and maybe toed a line of innocence … out of mind, out of sight … stand back … you have to leave … visiting hours are over.

VACANCY

Today, I am the caretaker for one of Brisbane's oldest evils: the retired gaol of Boggo Road. There are still a few walls, towers and buildings, but the horror is mostly landfill now, along with selected ghosts, as the developers move in. I am the caretaker, a sole security guard in a graveyard of macabre remains and a boneyard of expensive machinery. Today is Sunday, the day of rest, and this place *is* literally dead! John Howard was rolled yesterday; just another nightmare removed from the landscape the workers are dreaming now, sleeping the hangover of the neo-utopia. Today, I'm guarding the boneyard from the world and guarding the world from the graveyard, where art deco apartments will soon sprout like daisies, pushed up from a redundant kitchen of hell. *But the horror needn't fret!* Prestigious chimera is being built everywhere now … and there's no shortage of jobs in this age for a hard-working nightmare.

ANTEBELLUM

For Tom Morello

'An injury to one is an injury to all.'
– Industrial Workers of the World

I've been in Wellington for a couple of days in the midst of the Gulf War Redux; this war that keeps on fighting. It is back in business, and as far as the oil-wealthy are concerned, business is still GOOD. Journalists keep the heaven of media moguls happy, supplied with the dark-fish of body bags.

An arousing wind takes me walking through the streets of Wellington. Alexander Downer would soon announce from Canberra, that New Zealand's unwillingness to join the coalition would affect their economy. Why join a war on the slavery that is primarily driven on Wall Street?

Te Whanganui-a-Tara
the Great Harbour of Wellington, I drop a tear of respect
into your windy-lips,
forget the smite of *my* parliament … *they* do not speak for me.

My brother is probably packing his bags right now (and he was) to be a part of some battle, somewhere. And if he had fallen in the field, we'd never be told exactly where.

Lock and load!
DEATH is a classified institution.

I bought into an 'All YOU CAN EAT!' Chinese outlet and the crispy lemon chicken tasted *so* good! The two Māori brothers in front of me made the manager cry. (These guys together weigh at least 300 kilos!) The sign says, ALL YOU CAN EAT and these bro's will get their money's worth!

I like it here. I like seeing a black cop and a black shopkeeper and going into a pub and not feeling the threat of being alienated and being served by a black bartender, so foreign to my retina, in the wake of one of the British Empire's last grips before the age of neo-colonialism.

Aotearoa stands firm! The mighty Māori invented trench warfare. Why was it necessary to reinvent this wheel of further mass-destruction when the antebellum of another war had not even been planned, far into the recklessness from Aotearoa's want?

Right now, I feel safe in Aotearoa, because in this antebellum of time, the people here have Waitangi. And although it won't work for everyone, in this wake of war, Waitangi is still a treaty; a treaty in a free-market of succession, where sovereignty is not respected or often written off as collateral damage.

A wound to one of us is a wound to us all …

THE PATIENT

My dreams bite like a teething baby,
I am helpless to punish them;
like a parent, I wish my dreams to sleep softly,
25 mg of Dothep eases the monsters under the bed
through the ebb of night,
a derided slumber,
with calm sombre snoring,
blood pressure easing,
240 mg of Verapamil,
Swallow whole – do not crush or chew with food
EACH NIGHT I REPEAT THIS …
a praying mantis tickling one's brow
and not threatening,
Alphapress kicks in softly, 50 mg,
with a taste of Prazosin, 2 mg,
I'm done, lightly,
the house locked,
my family safe.
EACH NIGHT I REPEAT THIS …
with the prescribed mantra that I may become a praying mantis
in my dreams stepping lightly, insect-like, through shadows,
To just take one, once a day … as prescribed or when needed
treading softly,
APO-Diazepam, 5 mg if necessary,
not attacking or taking hold of me
and finally sleeping soundly in the reality of my medicated wake.

When the second stroke of midnight comes,
and I'm once again back in a ward, paralysed but
comfortable
with moon-milk bathing the sterile environment
on the ante-meridian run,
life will repeat itself
and what has not yet killed me
will just have to make me stronger …

THE BOOK, THE JUNGLE, THE JUDGEMENT

The Judge looks down on my client; a young Murri man,
looks down, looks down, *swear on the Bible* ... this poor kid?
He can hardly read a word of the Queen's English,
a victim of the Queen's pleasure, but this crazy old Judge,
this crazy old British ex-pat from the subcontinent,
he's willing to give this young brother bail,
but not until he condemns this poor kid's spirit,
grinds him into the dust of the courtroom,
and we've noted in the application that our client has never
been schooled,
but he's looked down upon, *illiteracy is no defence!*
And this crazy old Judge – he was known for his madness;
as mad as King George!
He rustles his wig and reads a few lines from his notes ...
my young brother, my client, looks at me, shrugs his shoulders,
our eyes meet and I motion for him to chill, to indulge in
this madness,
but I can't believe this crazy old Judge,
quoting Rudyard Kipling's *The Jungle Book*?!
He's going to squeeze this poor brother before he lets him go,
*Bail granted, but you better appreciate what I'm doing for you,
young man!*
So I walk my young brother down George Street and put
him on a bus,
back to his world from this jungle, back to the Mission
where he remains today,
in the Mission cemetery,
knife wound to the abdomen,
he never even had the chance to learn to read,

so he never picked up on what that crazy old Judge was
    trying to tell him,
in his condescending malice,
the madness of the jungle,
and his colonialist attire,
all for the hollow romanticism of Kipling.

GOING ROGUE

For Harri Kettunen

We launched before a hound-dog shore-break. I only wanted to wade in the waters where some of the prayers of animals are answered and basic instincts cleansed. I'll always be a dingo though, and stray from my own path. But, I'm not alone tonight, in the stomping grounds of my brother-in-law; a Finnish fox.

We howled: Kippis, *Kippis,* ***Kippis!*** On the wind-sheets of this night from the Pacific-blown avenues of Kings Beach, Caloundra, bellies full as the belly of the lunar-tide that reached a record high. It tore havoc down the coast where the rents are skyrocketing and the fantasies of financial drifters are hard-mouthed and sore in the gutters of streets, supposedly paved with gold.

Onshore blasts rocking and rolling us, winds as big as zeppelins, gusts as solid as lead … and even though we're in Caloundra, we're both in a mindset of Kashmir.

This Finnish fox and a rogue dingo, both bitten by love but never shy. The surf is up and we howl at the moon; a lunar face of beauty, glowing, un-judging goddess into a vagabond orbit.

Howl to the moon, howl to the moon, howl to the moon!

Tubes crashing and pandanus trees clapping! Apart from the moon goddess, they seemed our only audience; rogue clowns in a two-dog night.

'Kippis' is the Finnish word for 'Cheers'.

ELSEWHERE

'… we were all from somewhere else'
– Raymond Carver, 'What We Talk About
When We Talk About Love'

Dark jaded frost spawns elsewhere, away from the warm, temperate climates of our own comfort zones. I assume my waters to have no cholera and my soil; void of pestilence. Once upon a time, we were all refugees deep in the ranges of innocence. Our thoughts had no borders and eyes knew only indiscriminate pleasures in our midst, and we sort permission to enter another's boundary. Now, my neighbours do not look or smell like me, and for their sins they are not welcome to my secrets. Have you ever wondered who invented barbed wire? Was it a mistake? Can I now lock my door for keepsakes that are of little value to others?

Envelop my fear, and seal my mind, RETURN TO SENDER, all misguided views. The people down the street are denied access through my gate of closed assumptions; behind the greatest sum of lies hide the smallest fears. You can't watch my back as I refuse to watch yours. I am gridlocked humanity on the narrow road of time that grows smaller and less travelled every day. This is a logistical entrapment, a trail pockmarked with puddles. Adonis, to Narcissus, to Medusa – they all fall forward like dominoes. We will all die lonely in succession. We will refuse the prosperity to mirror one another as the truth lies in our murky reflections, unable to rewind to the black and white frame from which we developed our first glimpse of innocence.

In the end, we are made in the pure image of a model, from elsewhere …

EVERY POET NEEDS A PLACE TO CALL HOME ...

For Mandy Beaumont

Well, Kerouac left us dry with his drinking
and he died a much loved but lonely man,
Neal Cassady drove me as a wandering poet,
I had 'the walkabout' muse, and wanted for nothing;
didn't need a mortgage or a master plan.

But does a poet need a place to call home?
A poet should have a place to call home …

Too many poets have been packaged in unmarked graves,
too many poets have died while picking a bone,
too many poets don't want the 'white picket fence' dream,
but at the end of the road; every poet needs a home.

A poet needs a place to call home
A poet needs a place to call home
A poet needs a place to call home
A poet needs a place to call home …

Sylvia Plath wasn't so good in the kitchen,
and William Burroughs was content with a *Naked Lunch*,
Rimbaud was only good at cooking absinthe,
as homemakers, poets are a DIY destructive bunch,
but every poet needs a place to call home.

Yeah, every poet needs a place to call home
Every poet needs a place to call home
Every poet needs a place to call home
Every poet needs a place to call home …

NO NAKED FLAMES

I once met an old blackfulla who introduced himself as 'Ham Spoon', and the Ham Spoon I met lived his waking moments behind the dank grey veil of a bent cigarette.

Through the plume of smoke he filtered an ant-trail of words that illustrated the frailties of the world he'd encountered upon his winding journey of treasures and misfortunes.

We were comrades; uncle and nephew, and we were also a minority. The only two Aboriginal men in a rooming-house of scared men, from every warzone between Morocco and East Timor; now trying to find peace.

But Uncle Spoon and I were a curious thorn in the reconciliation of this Lucky Country. They just couldn't grasp the notion of our beings. The refugee status of two native sons on their own land; the front of our war was a mystery to them.

Hey boy … you got a smoke? was Uncle Ham's rough greeting into the day. *Uncle, you know I don't smoke!* But he had to ask; because the past, present and future of Aboriginal existence is always in a triumvirate state of flux.

Uncle Spoon would then launch the dawn with a story; as if he was acknowledging the soil beneath our feet, the moisture in our midst and the wind that carried his fluffy-grey beard of smoke.

Always hide your matches, boy … keep 'em dry! Even though I never carried matches either, he constantly lectured me about the dangers of exposing my anger to the world and to keep my fire guarded in a tinderbox where the harbouring naked flames were not a prerequesite of daily suvival.

He had surviving memories of giant albino kangaroo ghosts, brumbies that could not be tamed but only matched, the vengeful punches of tent-boxing gladiators, in times and torrents of a tide that swept up our country …

Uncle … you need to write your stories down! And for the first time I saw his face, the scars of life, his eyes dropping hard into the clasps of his weathered hands, arthritic crow-claws that matched his dark mulga walking stick.

These hands can only sign my name … they've never ever finished a sentence …

Endangered species;
Roman candles burning bright,
on brittle matchsticks

BUTTERFLIES FROM COLOMBIA ...

In the late afternoon on a freshly mowed lawn, I read the translated works from one of Colombia's most recognised poets, José Asunción Silva. He too was mused by butterflies, both dead and alive, to illustrate the beauty that can hatch from the chrysalis of the human condition. An invitation had just arrived for me to attend the world's largest poetry festival, in Medellín, Colombia. My mind narrowly missed the wonders that I could be experiencing in Silva's homeland; instead, I choke inspiration and think only of the danger that drug cartels can pose. I decide to meditate over Silva's poems in the cool of the garden, joined by white and yellow sulphurs kiting erratically between tufts of grass. What looks like a moth swoops into low view, playfully swanning with a couple of smaller sulphurs out from under a bush. Their antics remind me of Auden's words: *We must love one another or die ...* To be in love with life and cut down in the same light of day becomes of so many. Death threats are sour and abundant, whilst affection is short but sweet where you can find it. I race back to the computer and send my reply:

Thank you for your gracious invitation ... now, how do I get to Colombia?

ADDENDUM

'We must love one another or die'.
W.H. Auden, 'September 1, 1939'

When I see your picture
I think of your sweetness,
I'm reminded of ghosts who harbour grudges,
shadows that carry flesh
butterflies that yearn for more time,
love poems and death threats …

ACKNOWLEDGEMENTS

Poems from this collection have appeared in the following books and magazines, some of them as earlier versions: *Cordite Poetry Review*; *Overland*; *Blast*; *Hotel Bone* and *The Curse Words* (Vagabond Press).

The author would like to thank the following entities in their support and assistance: Queensland Writers Centre; New South Wales Writers Centre; Brisbane City Council; Japan Aerospace Exploration Agency; Booranga Writers Writers (Wagga Wagga); Hunter Writers Centre; Newcastle Art Gallery; the Northern Territory Writers Centre; Riddu Riđđu Festival (Norway); Utan Kayu (Indonesia); Jenny Fraser (CyberTribe); Leah Flanagan Band; Copyright Agency; Australian Broadcasting Corporation; 98.9FM and Brisbane Indigenous Media Association; Felicity Plunkett and University of Queensland Press.

First published 2014 by University of Queensland Press
PO Box 6042, St Lucia, Queensland 4067 Australia
Reprinted 2015, 2019 (twice), 2022

www.uqp.com.au
reception@uqp.com.au

Cover design by Josh Durham / Design By Committee
Cover photograph by elena the wise/Bigstock.com
Typeset in 11.5/14 pt Adobe Garamond by Post Pre-press Group, Brisbane
Printed in Australia by McPherson's Printing Group

National Library of Australia cataloguing-in-publication data
is available at http://catalogue.nla.gov.au

ISBN
978 0 7022 5327 0 (pbk)
978 0 7022 5428 4 (epdf)
978 0 7022 5249 1 (epub)
978 0 7022 5430 7 (Kindle)

University of Queensland Press uses papers that are natural, renewable and recyclable products made from wood grown in well-managed forests and other controlled sources. The logging and manufacturing processes conform to the environmental regulations of the country of origin.

FSC www.fsc.org MIX Paper | Supporting responsible forestry FSC® C001695